Foreword.

This volume is a sequel to our previously published and now widely used Easy Classics To Moderns and More Easy Classics To Moderns (Numbers 17 and 27 in the Music for Millions Series). The piano literature of nearly three centuries is represented by these original compositions of medium grade difficulty. All selections are in their original form, neither re-arranged nor simplified. They are set in approximately chronological order.

CLASSICS TO MODERNS

In The Intermediate Grades

Compiled and Edited by Denes Agay

Marks of phrasing and expression are often editorial additions especially in the music of the pre-classical period. These signs were added for a quicker and easier understanding of the structure and mood of the compositions. They are to be considered as suggestions rather than rigid directions. Students, teachers and all pianists should find these original piano works valuable for study, recital, sight reading or just inspired musical entertainment of the highest caliber.

The Publisher.

Order No. AM 41617
International Standard Book Number: 0.8256.4037.7
Library Of Congress Catalog Card Number: 62-22540

Music Sales America

Distributed By
HAL•LEONARD® CORPORATION
7777 W. Bluemound Rd. P.O. Box 13819 Milwaukee, WI 53213

Contents

ABOUT STRANGE LANDS AND PEOPLE ..... Robert Schumann 84
ADAGIO *from Toccata No. 11* ..... Georg Muffat 10
AIR ..... Henry Purcell 4
ALBUM LEAF ..... César Franck 103
ALLA POLACCA ..... Carl Philipp Emanuel Bach 54
ALLEGRO (A Major) ..... Wilhelm Friedemann Bach 50
ALLEGRO GIOCOSO (F Major) ..... Joseph Haydn 64
ALLEGRO SCHERZANDO ..... Joseph Haydn 58
ALLEMANDE (A minor) ..... Georg Friedrich Händel 35
ARIA ..... Johann Kuhnau 20
BAGATELLE (Op. 119, No. 11) ..... Ludwig van Beethoven 71
BAGATELLE (Op. 119, No. 5) ..... Ludwig van Beethoven 72
BALLET ANGLOIS ..... Johann Kaspar Ferdinand Fischer 11
BOURREE I *from French Overture* ..... Johann Sebastian Bach 33
BOURREE II *from French Overture* ..... Johann Sebastian Bach 34
BRISK GAME ..... Dmitri Kabalevsky 136
CANZONI DI DANZA ..... Bernardo Pasquini 12
CAPRICCIO ..... Domenico Scarlatti 18
CHACONNE (G Major) ..... Georg Friedrich Händel 40
CHANSON SANS PAROLES (Op. 40, No. 2) ..... Jan Sibelius 130
CHILDREN'S PIECE (Op. 72, No. 1) ..... Felix Mendelssohn 90
COURANTE (F Major) ..... Georg Friedrich Händel 37
COWHERD'S SONG, THE *from Op. 17* ..... Edvard Grieg 108
DANCE WITH A BELL ..... Vladimir Rebikoff 127
DAWN ..... Béla Bartok 160
ELFIN DANCE ..... Edvard Grieg 110
FANTASIA (D Major) ..... Carl Philipp Emanuel Bach 53
FANTASIE (G Minor) ..... Georg Philipp Telemann 43
FARMER'S DAUGHTERS ..... Heitor Villa-Lobos 146
FIVE ECOSSAISES ..... Franz Schubert 80
FOUR HUNGARIAN FOLK TUNES ..... Béla Bartók 155
1. COURTING SONG 155
2. PLAY TUNE 156
3. STARS, SHINE BRIGHTLY 158
4. DRINKING SONG 159
FROM A STORY BOOK ..... Robert Volkmann 112
FROLIC (Op. 17, No. 12) ..... Max Reger 124
FUGHETTA ..... Domenico Zipoli 13
FUGHETTA (G Major) ..... Johann Sebastian Bach 30
FUN AT HOME *from "The Adventures of Ivan"* ..... Aram Khatchaturian 148
GAVOTTA ..... Arcangelo Corelli 14
GAVOTTE *from French Suite No. 5* ..... Johann Sebastian Bach 32
GERMAN DANCE (G Major) ..... Joseph Haydn 60
GIGUE *from Suite No. 11* ..... Georg Friedrich Händel 42
GIGUE EN RONDEAU ..... Jean Philippe Rameau 48
GOODNESS! ..... Heitor Villa-Lobos 147
GYMNOPEDIE NO. 3 ..... Erik Satie 134
HORNPIPE ..... Henry Purcell 6
HORSEMAN, THE ..... Dmitri Kabalevsky 140
IMPROVISATION ..... Robert Schumann 87
INTERMEZZO ..... Theodor Kirchner 107
INVENTION (C Major) ..... Johann Sebastian Bach 28

IVAN IS ILL *from "The Adventures of Ivan"* ..... Aram Khatchaturian 150
JIGG ..... Jeremiah Clarke 8
JUGGLER, THE ..... Johann Philipp Kirnberger 55
KAMARINSKAIA (Russian Folk Tune) ..... Peter Ilyitch Tchaikovsky 104
KUKLA (The Russian Doll) ..... Vladimir Rebikoff 128
L'AUGUSTE ..... Carl Philipp Emanuel Bach 51
LA DIANE ..... Francois Couperin 21
LA FLORENTINE ..... Francois Couperin 22
LA JOYEUSE ..... Jean Philippe Rameau 46
LAMENT ..... Zoltán Kodály 154
LITTLE PRELUDE (C Minor) ..... Johann Sebastian Bach 26
MARCH *from Suite No. 5* ..... Henry Purcell 7
MAZURKA (Op. 67, No. 2) ..... Frédéric Chopin 98
MENUETT ..... Gottfried Heinrich Stölzel 24
MINUET (C Minor) ..... Joseph Haydn 62
MINUET AND TRIO *from Viennese **Sonatina No. 1*** ..... Wolfgang Amadeus Mozart 68
MUSETTE *from English Suite No. 2* ..... Johann Sebastian Bach 39
NORSE SONG ..... Robert Schumann 85
NOVELETTE ..... Dmitri Kabalevsky 138
ON THE PLAYGROUND ..... Nikolai Rakov 152
PARADE OF THE GRASSHOPPERS ..... Serge Prokofieff 143
PASSEPIED ..... Georg Philipp Telemann 38
POLKA ..... Peter Ilyitch Tchaikovsky 105
POLONAISE ..... Wilhelm Friedemann Bach 59
PRELUDE (Op. 28, No. 6) ..... Frédéric Chopin 94
PRELUDE (Op. 28, No. 7) ..... Frédéric Chopin 95
PRELUDE (Op. 28, No. 4) ..... Frédéric Chopin 96
PRELUDE (Op. 28, No. 20) ..... Frédéric Chopin 97
PRELUDE (Op. 11, No. 4) ..... Alexander Scriabine 129
PRELUDE ..... Dmitri Shostakovich 142
ROMANCE ..... Reinhold Glière 132
RUSTIC SONG ..... Robert Schumann 86
SAEBYGGA (Song of the North) ..... Edvard Grieg 109
SARABAND *from Suite No. 2* ..... Henry Purcell 5
SCHERZO ..... Johann Nepomuk Hummel 88
SEA PIECE (Op. 55, No. 5) ..... Edward MacDowell 120
SIX VARIATIONS ON A SWISS SONG ..... Ludwig van Beethoven 74
SOLFEGGIETTO ..... Carl Philipp Emanuel Bach 56
SONATA (G Major) ..... Domenico Scarlatti 15
SONG OF THE NORTH (Saebygga) ..... Edvard Grieg 109
SONG WITHOUT WORDS (Op. 19, No. 4) ..... Felix Mendelssohn 92
TARANTELLA ..... Michael Glinka 100
THREE LÄNDLER ..... Franz Schubert 78
THREE WALTZES ..... Franz Schubert 82
TO A WILD ROSE *from "Woodland Sketches"* ..... Edward MacDowell 118
TOCCATA ..... Leonardo Leo 16
TRIO *for Menuett by Stölzel* ..... Johann Sebastian Bach 25
TWO BRAZILIAN CHILDREN'S SONGS ..... Heitor Villa-Lobos 146
VALSES POETICOS ..... Enrique Granados 114
VIENNESE SONATINA NO. 1 (*First Movement*) ..... Wolfgang Amadeus Mozart 66
WALTZ (K. 567, No. 5) ..... Wolfgang Amadeus Mozart 70
WALTZ (Op. 39, No. 9) ..... Johannes Brahms 102
WALTZ (Op. 39, No. 8) ..... Peter Ilyitch Tchaikovsky 106

Air

Henry Purcell
(1659-1695)

Allegretto

Saraband

Henry Purcell

Hornpipe

Allegro

Henry Purcell

March

Henry Purcell

Jigg

Jeremiah Clarke
(1669–1707)

dim.
p
mf
p
cresc.
dim.
mf
f
rit.

Adagio

from Toccata No. 11

George Muffat
(1645–1704)

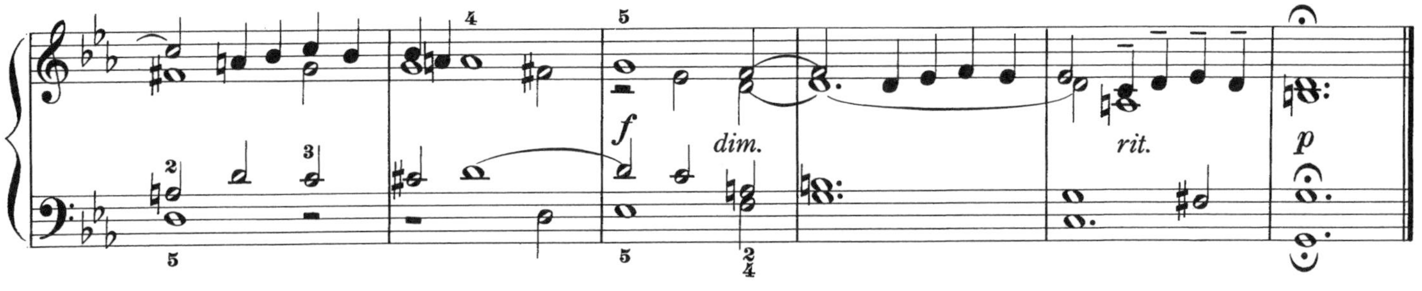

Ballet Anglois

Johann Kaspar Ferdinand Fischer
(1650–1746)

* *Play all eighth notes staccato*

Canzoni di Danza

Bernardo Pasquini
(1637–1710)

* *Play all eighth notes staccato*

Fughetta

Domenico Zipoli
(1688-1726)

Allegro energico

Gavotta

Arcangelo Corelli
(1658-1713)

Sonata

Domenico Scarlatti
(1685–1757)

Toccata

Leonardo Leo
(1694-1744)

Moderato

crescendo
crescendo
p subito
allargando
crescendo

Capriccio

Domenico Scarlatti
(1685-1757)

Allegro moderato

cresc.

Aria

Johann Kuhnau
(1660–1722)

La Diane

Francois Couperin
(1668–1733)

La Florentine

Francois Couperin

Allegretto con tenerezza

* *Original time signature* 12/16

poco rit.
a tempo
p

Menuett

From J.S.Bach's "Little Note Book
for Wilhelm Friedemann Bach"

Allegro giústo

Gottfried Heinrich Stölzel
(1690-1749)

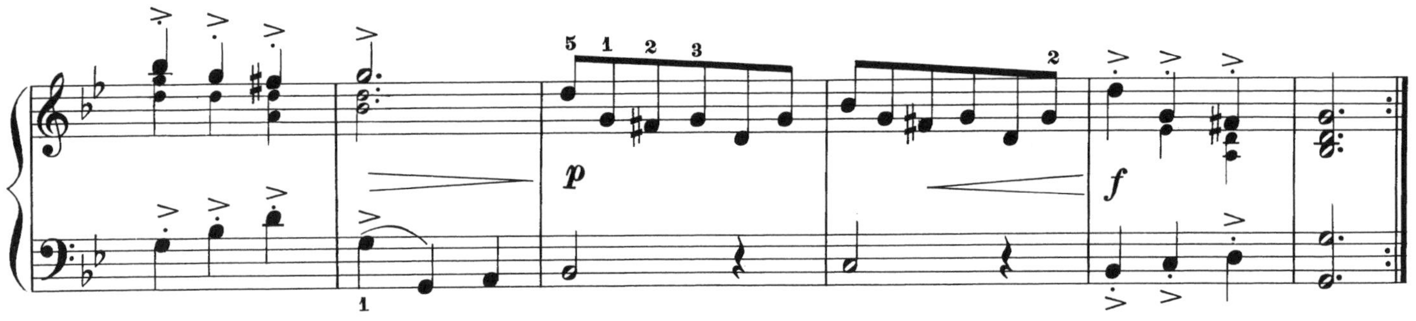

Trio*

Johann Sebastian Bach
(1685-1750)

Andantino espressivo

Repeat Menuett

* *Bach wrote this Trio to follow and be part of the preceding Menuett*

Little Prelude

Con moto

Johann Sebastian Bach

mf
dim.
p
cresc.
f

Invention

Johann Sebastian Bach

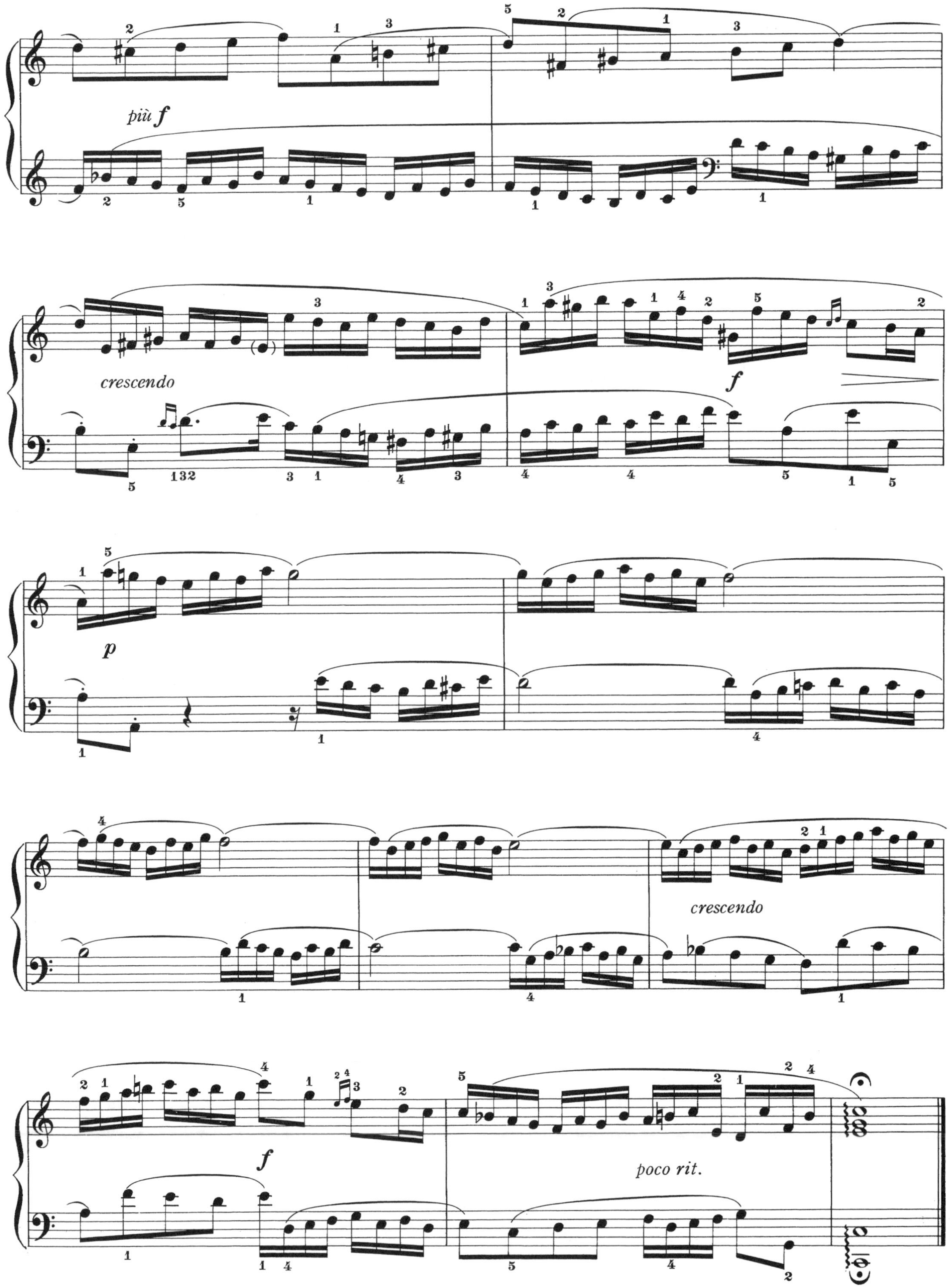
più f
crescendo
f
p
crescendo
f
poco rit.

Fughetta

Johann Sebastian Bach

Allegretto

f
L. H.
rit.

Gavotte

from French Suite No. 5

Johann Sebastian Bach

Bourrée I

from French Overture

Johann Sebastian Bach

Bourrée II

from French Overture

Johann Sebastian Bach

Allemande

Georg Friedrich Händel
(1685–1759)

Andante

mf
dim.
p
cresc.
f
p
f
dim.
cresc.
rit.

Courante

Georg Friedrich Händel

Passepied

Georg Philipp Telemann
(1681-1767)

Vivo

Musette

from English Suite No. 2

Johann Sebastian Bach
(1685-1750)

Andantino grazioso

Chaconne

Theme And Six Variations

Georg Friedrich Händel

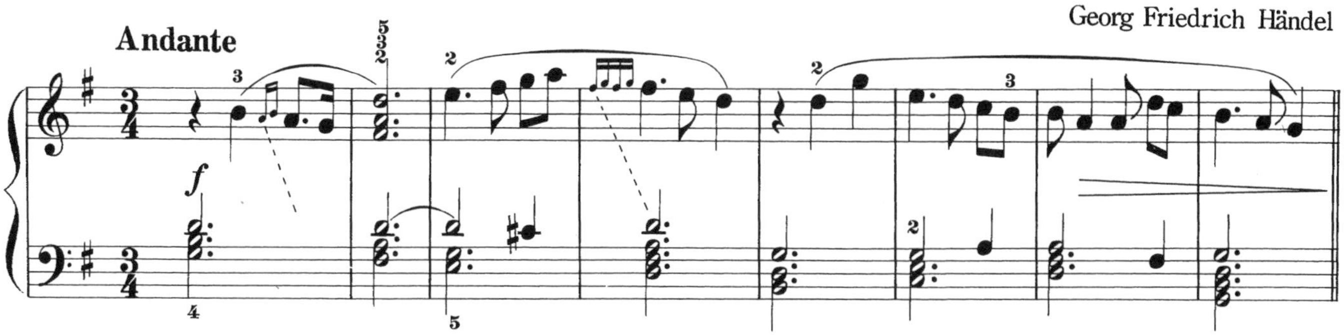

Var. 1

Var. 2

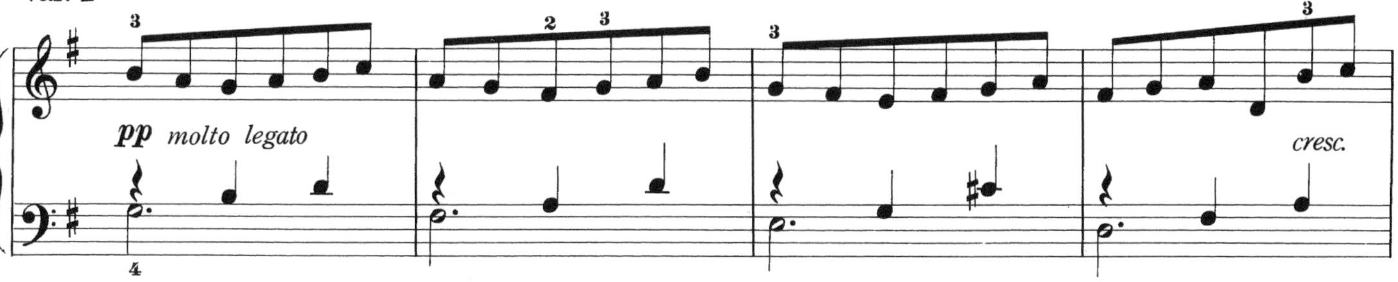

Var. 3

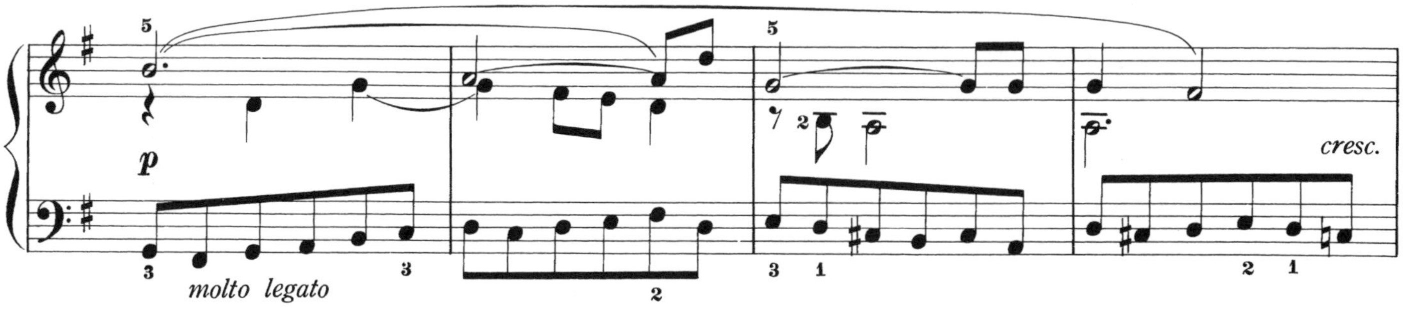

dim.
Var. 4
f pesante
Var. 5
p
cresc.
mp
dim.
p
Var. 6
f
sempre f
rit.

Gigue

Georg Friedrich Händel

Vivace

Fantasie

Georg Philipp Telemann
(1681-1767)

p
legato
mf
p
f
p
f
mp cantabile

p subito
crescendo
f
allarg.
a tempo
f
mp
f
allargando
ff

La Joyeuse

Jean Philippe Rameau
(1683-1764)

mf
f
p
mp
p
crescendo
f
poco rit.

Gigue En Rondeau

Jean-Philippe Rameau
(1683–1764)

Fine
p
crescendo
f
mf
dim. sempre
p
D. S.
al Fine

Allegro

Wilhelm Friedemann Bach
(1710–1784)

L'Auguste

Carl Philipp Emanuel Bach
(1714–1788)

Andante cantabile

p
crescendo
mf
p
f
R.H.

Fantasia

Carl Philipp Emanuel Bach
(1714–1788)

Alla Polacca

Carl Philipp Emanuel Bach

The Juggler

Johann Philipp Kirnberger
(1721-1783)

Allegro moderato

Solfeggietto

Carl Philipp Emanuel Bach

Allegro Scherzando

Joseph Haydn
(1732–1809)

Polonaise

Wilhelm Friedemann Bach
(1710 – 1784)

Moderato

German Dance

Allegro con brio

Joseph Haydn

Trio
p
mf
f
mp
p
mf
dim.
p
D. C. al Fine

Minuet

Joseph Haydn

poco rit.
a tempo
p
mf
p
f
p
mf
p
crescendo
mf
ff

Allegro Giocoso

Joseph Haydn
(1732 – 1809)

f
p
f
p
f
mp cresc.
f
mf
p
f
f
mf
p
poco rit.
Da Capo
senza replica

Viennese Sonatina No.1

First Movement

Wolfgang Amadeus Mozart
(1756-1791)

Allegro brillante

cresc.

Minuet and Trio

from Viennese Sonatina No.1

Wolfgang Amadeus Mozart

Trio
p
crescendo
p
p
poco rit.
a tempo
p
p
f
mf
p
Menuetto da capo

Waltz

Wolfgang Amadeus Mozart
(K.567, No. 5)

Allegretto

Bagatelle

(Op. 119, No. 11)

Ludwig van Beethoven
(1770–1827)

Bagatelle

(Op. 119, No. 5)

Ludwig van Beethoven

mf
non legato
crescen-
-do
mf
più f
non legato
f
mf
più f
f
f
f
f p subito
pp

Six Variations On A Swiss Song

Theme

Ludwig van Beethoven

Andante con moto

Var. I

Var. II
mf
mf
mf
f
Var. III
Minore
sempre p e legato
p
mp
p
pp

Var. IV

Maggiore

Var. V

p
mf
p
Var. VI
ff
p
ff
p
R.H.
ff
p
dim.
pp

Three Ländler

Franz Schubert
(1797–1828)

1

2

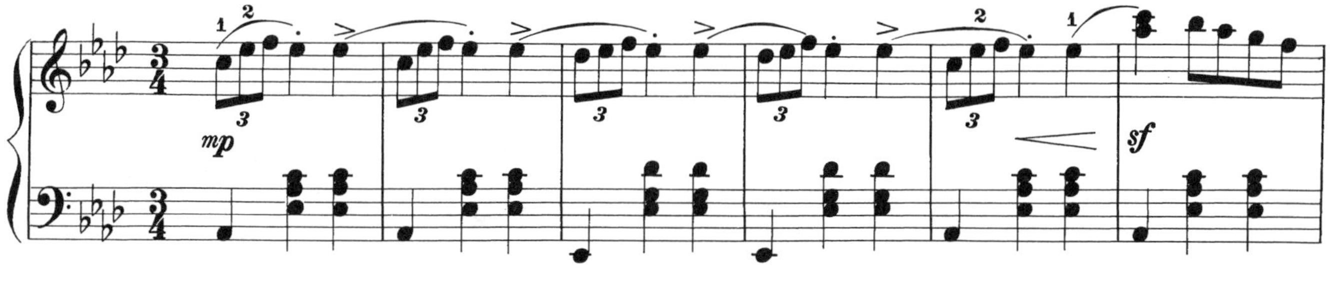

mf
mf
f
3
p
mp
f
p
f
p

Five Ecossaises

Franz Schubert

Animato

1

2

3

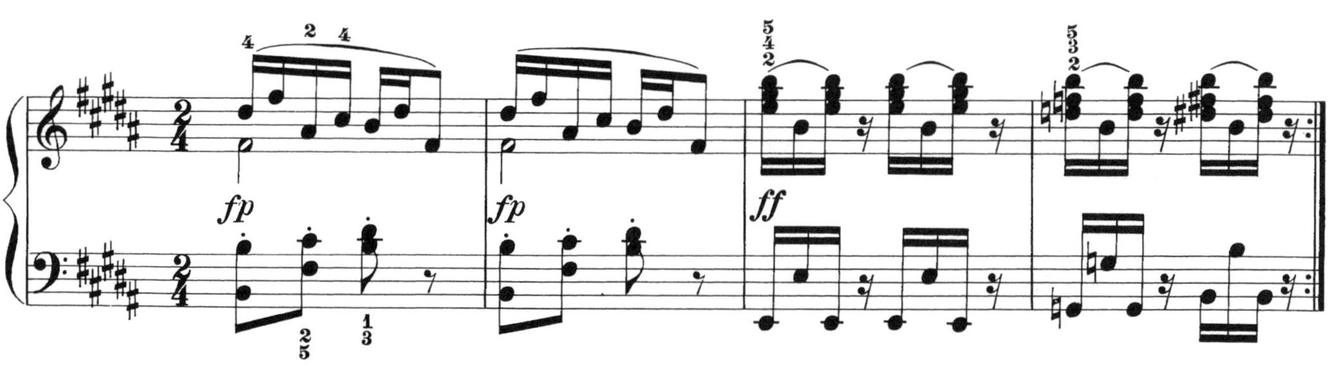

pp
ff
4
p
mf
p
fz
p
f
5
p
p
f
p
f

Three Waltzes

Franz Schubert

Vivo
3
p
p
mf
1.
2.

About Strange Lands and People

Robert Schumann
(1810 -1856)

Norse Song

Greeting to G*

Robert Schumann

* *Niels W. Gade, friend of Schumann*

Rustic Song

Robert Schumann

Improvisation*

Robert Schumann

* On a theme-fragment by Beethoven (Prison Terzett from "Fidelio")

Scherzo

Johann Nepomuk Hummel
(1787 - 1837)

p
crescendo
f
dimin.
poco rit.
a tempo
mf
dim. sempre
pp
poco accel.

Children's Piece

(Op. 72, No. 1)

Felix Mendelssohn
(1809-1847)

Allegro moderato

crescendo
dim.

Song Without Words

(Op. 19, No. 4)

Felix Mendelssohn

mf
p
rfz
p
crescendo
ff
dim.
ritard.
p
a tempo
pp
p

Prelude

(Op. 28, No. 6)

Frédéric Chopin
(1810-1849)

Prelude

(Op. 28, No. 7)

Frédéric Chopin

Prelude

(Op. 28, No. 4)

Frédéric Chopin

Prelude

(Op. 28, No. 20)

Largo

Frédéric Chopin

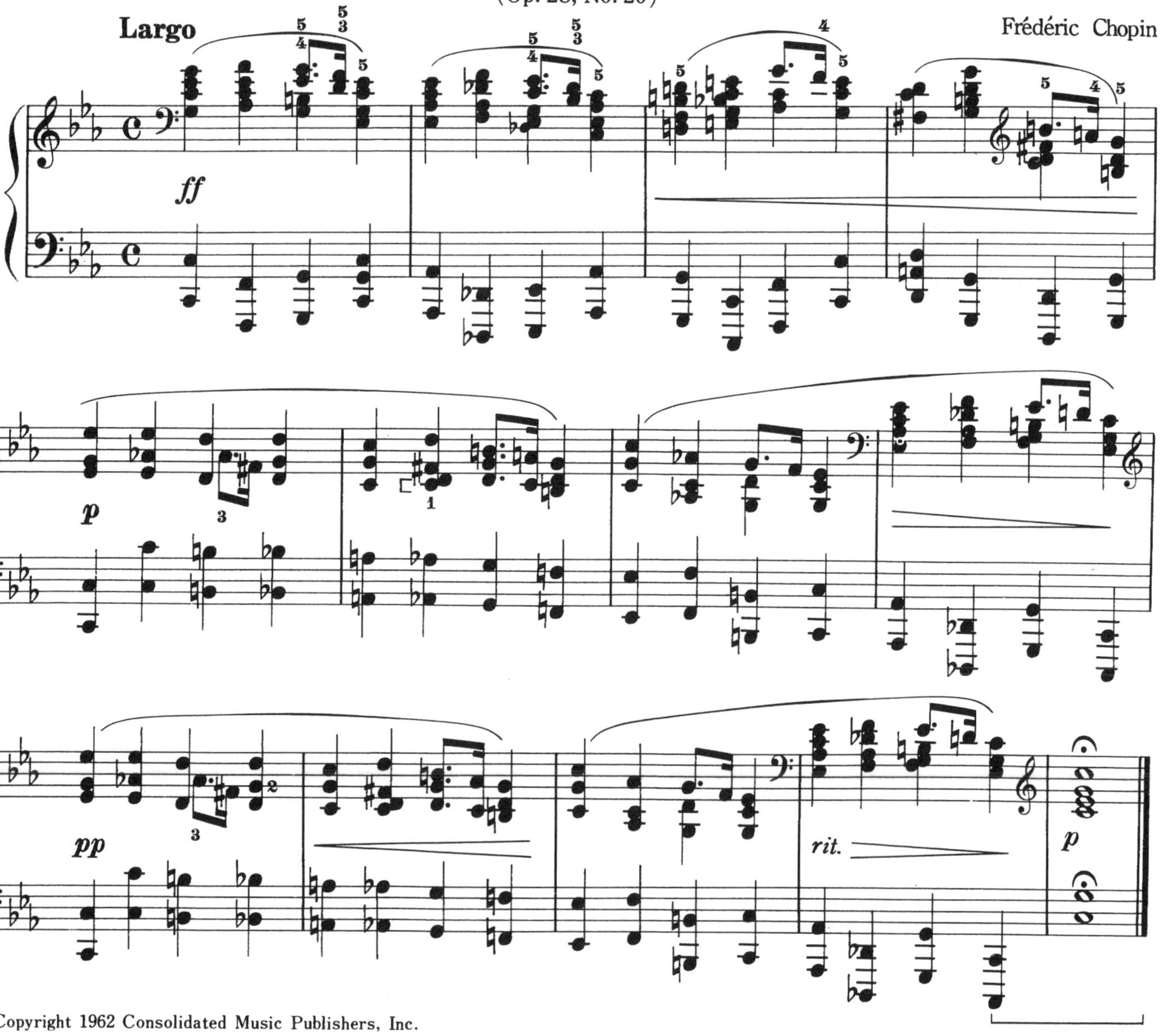

Mazurka

(Op. 67, No. 2)

Frédéric Chopin,

8va
poco cresc.
Tempo I
poco rit.
cresc.
poco rit.

Tarantella

Michael Glinka
(1804-1857)

p legato
pp
pp
mf
p
pp
f
p
f
poco rit.
D. C.

Waltz

(Op. 39, No. 9)

Johannes Brahms
(1833-1897)

Con moto espressivo

Album Leaf

César Franck
(1822–1890)

Kamarinskaia

(Russian Folk Tune)

Peter Ilyitch Tchaikovsky
(1840-1893)

Polka

Peter Ilyitch Tchaikovsky

Waltz

Peter Ilyitch Tchaikovsky

Intermezzo

Theodor Kirchner
(1823-1903)

The Cowherd's Song

(from Op. 17)

Edvard Grieg
(1843-1907)

Song Of The North

(Saebygga)

(from Op. 17)

Edvard Grieg

Elfin Dance

Edvard Grieg

cresc.

From A Story Book

Robert Volkmann
(1815-1883)

Allegro giocos

poco rit.
a tempo
p
crescendo
f
mf
crescendo sempre
f
rit.
dim.

Valses Poeticos

Enrique Granados
(1867–1916)

Allegro humoristico

Allegretto elegante

3

Quasi ad libitum (sentimental)

4

dim.
poco rall.
pp
mf a tempo
pp
mf
cresc.
con passione
dim.
ten.
p
f con molto espressione
decresc.
mp
rall.
mf a tempo
dim.
p rall. molto

To A Wild Rose

from " Woodland Sketches"

Edward MacDowell
(1861-1908)

With simple tenderness

a tempo
f
diminish
rit.
p
p
mp slightly marked
p
pp
ppp

Sea Piece

("A merry song, a chorus brave...")

Lively, in changing moods

Edward MacDowell

rit.
a tempo
pp
Somewhat slower
pp
f
passionately
rit.
a tempo
pp
slightly rit.
Slower, with great tenderness
mf
dim.
pp

a tempo
f
f
passionately
pp
Tempo I°
crescendo
pp

boisterously
ff
rit.
ff
pp
rit.
Slower, with great tenderness
pp
a tempo
pp
rit.
dim.
ppp

Frolic

(Op. 17, No. 12)

Max Reger
(1873-1916)

poco a poco dim. e rit.

a tempo
crescendo

Dance With A Bell

Vladimir Rebikoff
(1866-1920)

Kukla
The Russian Doll

Vladimir Rebikoff

Prelude No.4

(Op. 11, No. 4)

Alexander Scriabine
(1872-1915)

Chanson Sans Paroles

(Op. 40, No. 2)

Jan Sibelius
(1865 – 1957)

Andantino

mp
p
crescendo
p
dolce
p
dim.

Romance

Reinhold Glière
(1875-1956)

cresc.
f
dim.
rit.
a tempo
p
mf
rit.
dim.
p

Gymnopedie No. 3

Erik Satie
(1866 – 1925)

p
L.H.
L.H.
p
pp L.H.
pp

Brisk Game

Dmitri Kabalevsky
(1904-)

Allegro assai e marcato

cresc.
f
f
p
poco a poco cresc.
ff
sf
sf

Novelette

Dmitri Kabalevsky

sempre cresc.
ff
mf
p
pp
p
pp
p
rit. e dim. al fine
ppp

The Horseman

Dmitri Kabalevsky

Allegro molto

cresc.

Prelude

Dmitri Shostakovich
(1906-)

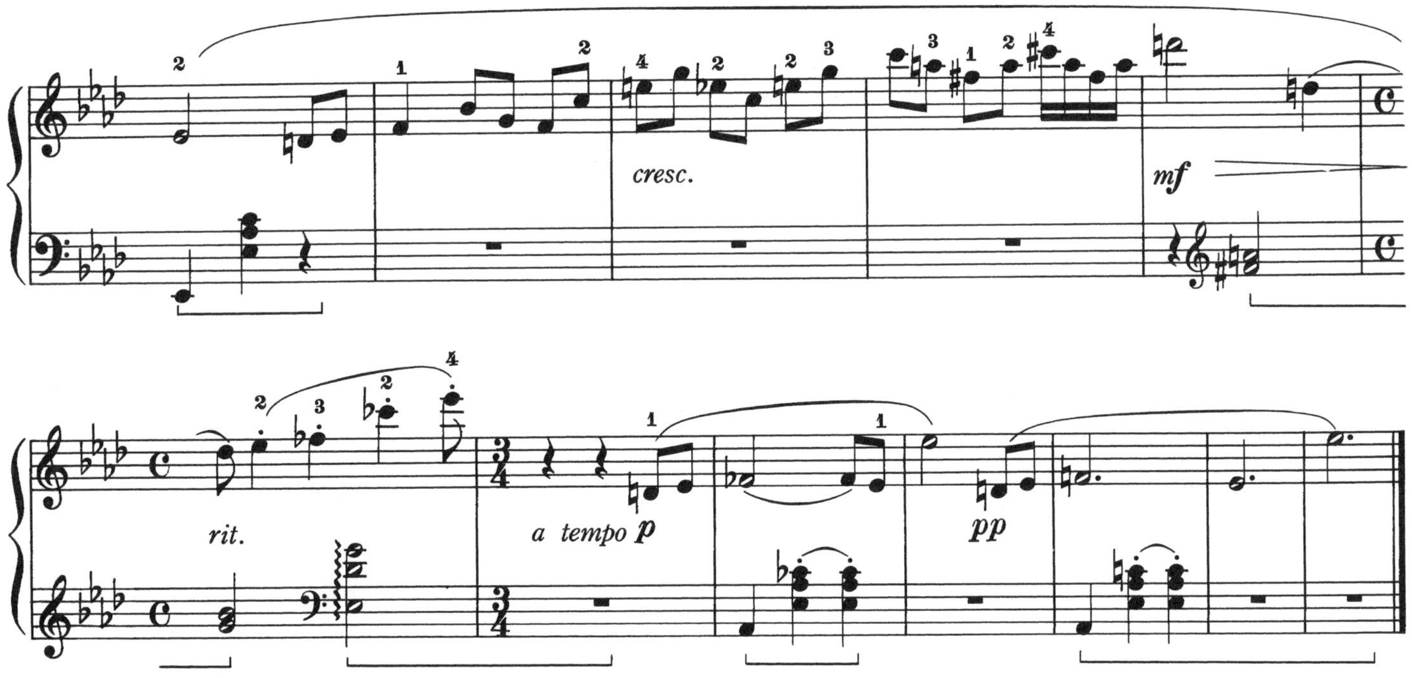

Parade Of The Grasshoppers

Serge Prokofieff
(1891-1953)

poco meno mosso
cresc.
mf
p
mp
p
f

dim.
poco rit.
Tempo I
p
cresc.
p
mf
f

Two Brazilian Children's Songs

from "Guia Prático"

1. Farmers' Daughters

Heitor Villa-Lobos
(1881-1959)

2. Goodness!

Fun At Home

from "The Adventures of Ivan"

Aram Khatchaturian
(1903-)

Allegro moderato

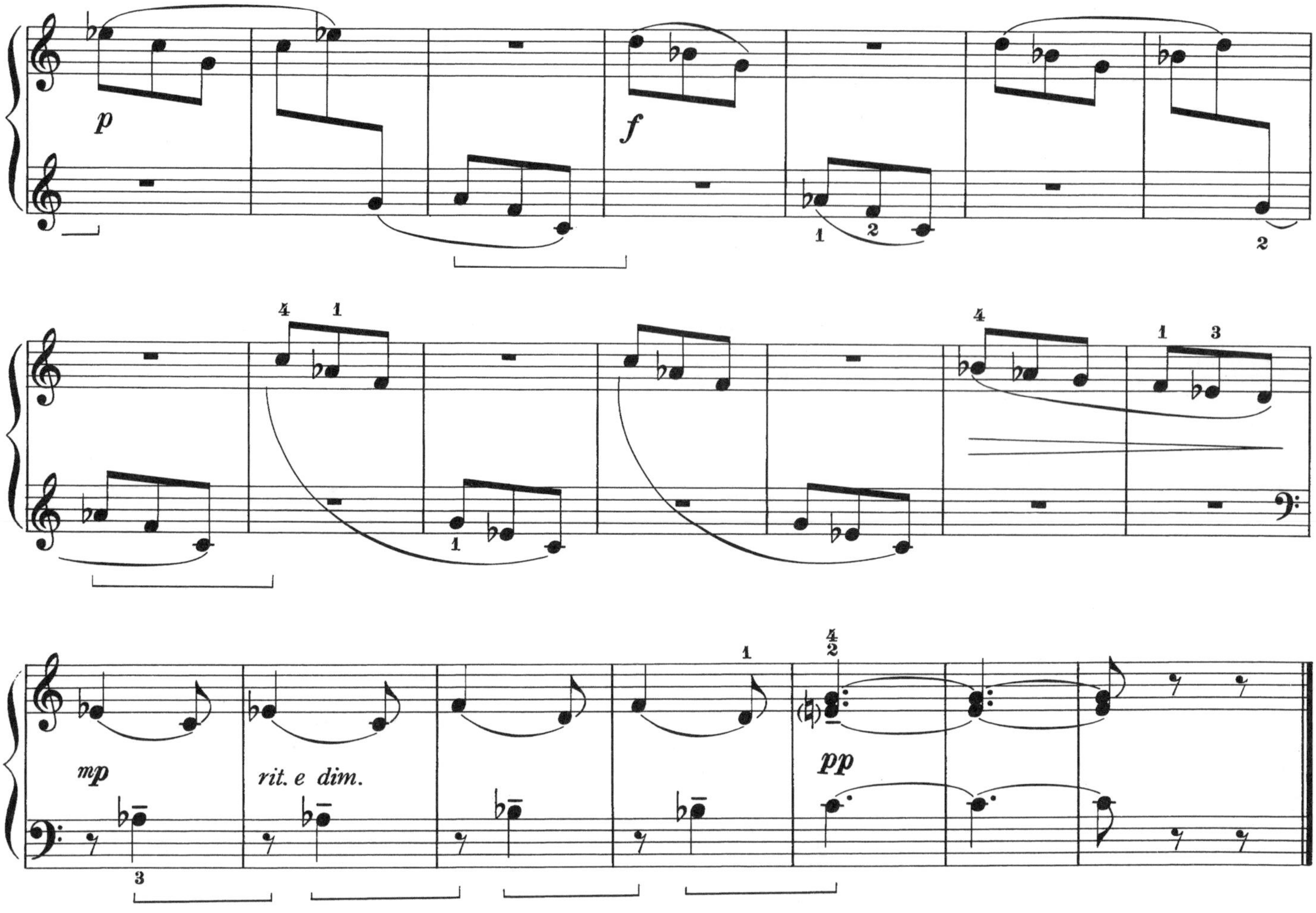

Ivan Is Ill

from "The Adventures of Ivan"

Aram Khatchaturian

Lento espressivo

f
p
f
mf
p
p
pp

On The Playground

Nikolai Rakov
(1908-)

f
mf
dim.
p
mf
p
rit.
f
8

Lament

Zoltán Kodály
(1882-)

Four Hungarian Folk Tunes

1.Courting Song

Béla Bartók
(1881-1945)

Allegro non troppo

2. Play Tune

Allegro
f
sempre legato
f grazioso
poco cresc.
dim.
p rit.
sempre legato
mf a tempo

f
p
p dolce
poco rit.
mp
a tempo
cresc. sempre
rit.
f
a tempo
p
ritenuto
p

3. Stars, Shine Brightly

4. Drinking Song

Dawn

Béla Bartók